1 Dec 06

Life without Timesheets
The freedom to charge what you are worth

Life without Timesheets

The freedom to charge what you are worth

Hugh Williams FCA

St Edward's Press Ltd

ABOUT THE AUTHOR

Hugh Williams has been a chartered accountant for over 35 years.
In 1973 Hugh set up HM Williams, an award-winning accountancy firm
(*the Daily Telegraph* Customer Service Award and the Butterworth Tolley
Award for best tax team in a small- to medium-sized business) that is now
renowned for its customer-focused approach.

Hugh was first published in 1988 with *The Private Company Secretary's
Manual* (CCH Wolters Kluwer), a bestseller on company law. Since then
he has written numerous other books, including *The Small Practice Tax
Guide* (with Robert Maas for the ICAEW's Tax Faculty) and a series of
acclaimed titles for Lawpack Publishing, including most recently, *Proper
Coffee and Other Ways to Grow Your Business*.

In addition to his writing work and running HM Williams, Hugh
is managing director of St Edward's Press, a publishing company that
operates under the credo 'An Independent and Different Approach'.

Hugh can be contacted at info@stedwardspress.co.uk

First published in 2006 by
St Edward's Press Ltd
Court House, The Crescent
Crapstone, Yelverton
Devon PL20 7PS
www.stedwardspress.co.uk

© St Edward's Press Ltd

ISBN 0-9554188-0-1

Typeset in ITC Charter
Printed in Great Britain by Lithocraft

CONTENTS

FOREWORD

Most of the readers of this book will not have heard of its author, Hugh Williams, before. This in itself shows the power of a good title and a good idea. This book, though, is more than just a good idea. It addresses a subject – replacing timesheets with fixed fees – about which I know Hugh feels passionately. Indeed he was lecturing about just this subject when I first met him through the auspices of the Institute of Chartered Accountants' Tax Faculty in 2001. I have since encouraged others to follow his lead; I have also quoted Hugh and his views when giving lectures around the country myself.

I well recall the genuine thrill I received when Hugh's firm won the Butterworth Tolley award for best tax team in a small to medium-sized practice; I was on the judging panel and had stressed to my fellow judges the importance of encouraging innovative practices like Hugh's. Hugh is living proof that you're never too old to learn or to change. Although he started his professional life in a conventional practice that worked with timesheets, he subsequently realised that this was not the best way to run a modern practice, and is now keen to help other firms to learn how and why they would benefit from adopting his 21st-century approach to billing.

Hugh's passion, pragmatism and commercial approach all come across loud and clear in his writing. If after reading this book you are not convinced of the logic of following Hugh's lead, it will not be because you couldn't follow his train of thought. Indeed you may want to take a good, long, hard look at whether you have merely rearranged your prejudices rather than considered his ideas with an open mind.

One final thought: I know through the research, mentoring and consulting work I do with professional firms that the ground is shifting. There has been a steady increase in the number of firms that offer fixed fees and that promise their clients that there will be no surprise bills. I run an online blog through which I share accountants' secrets with business owners and the self-employed, and two of the most common complaints I hear in response are about advisers who will not quote a fee in advance, and those who bill more than the client was expecting. Some advisers take the attitude that it's inevitable some clients will complain, and so continue to do things 'the way they've always been done'. Hugh's contention – and mine – is that the world has changed and those advisers who change with it will get a bigger share of the work that's out there.

No longer is it true to say that 'Everyone uses timesheets – clients don't have a choice'. Clients *do* have a choice and increasing numbers are exercising their right to appoint advisers who deal with them using the far fairer and, ultimately, more profitable approach for which Hugh is such a great advertisement.

Mark Lee FCA CTA (Fellow)
Chairman of the Tax Faculty of the Institute of Chartered Accountants in England & Wales 2003–2005

For more details on Mark's work, visit www.BookMarkLee.co.uk

Time for a new approach

Although I find it difficult to offer a convenient one-line explanation of what the 'New Approach' is that underpins the advice in this book, it is very easy to understand once you spot it – so let me begin by telling you about the first time I consciously recognised an example of it in action.

In 1994 my wife, Alice, and I celebrated 20 years of marriage. I decided that to mark the event I would take her to the Savoy Hotel in London. (Both Alice's and my parents had stayed there, and my in-laws were married in the chapel behind the hotel during World War II.) I made all the bookings and when the day for our trip finally came round, we headed off from Surrey with the aim of reaching 'one of the best hotels in the world' shortly after noon, in comfortable time for lunch.

But the best laid schemes of mice and men gang aft agley. The traffic in London was dreadful and held us up for an hour or more, so we were very late in arriving. Now this delay annoyed me greatly – our special time together was going wrong from the very beginning. I had planned it pretty well over the preceding months and here it was being derailed before it had even begun.

We eventually drove into the Savoy forecourt, very late and pretty upset. But, as I brought the car to a halt, three people came out to meet us: one to welcome us and escort us to the reception desk, another to collect our luggage from the boot and a third to drive the car away and park it for us. As we walked in through the hotel's revolving doors, a tide of care seemed to embrace and overwhelm us, to take away our upset, to cosset us as (in my view) only the Savoy can. We both relished the attention the hotel's staff lavished on us – and all my angst faded away.

When we left two days later, after 48 hours of supreme cosseting, I found myself saying that I wanted our accountancy practice to be to our profession what the Savoy is to the hotel industry. Yes, this was a most ambitious thought but their example had been just exceptional. We had felt really cared for throughout our visit. Yes, we had paid handsomely for the care, but we still felt our stay had been good value for money. From that point on, I wanted to copy the Savoy's approach in the way we at HM Williams treated our clients.

But if we want to be the best, we have to make a plan to be the best. If we just express this wish but do nothing about it, then nothing will happen – we have to take action. My hope is that in this book you will find some ideas that you will be able to develop and run with, and which will help you achieve your ambitions for your practice.

If, as a result of our efforts, we can reach the heights that the Savoy has reached, the world will not just come to us in numbers, but everyone will look on us as being *the* place to do business with – the standard against which all others are judged. Now while we would never pretend that our small practice has achieved this level of success, within eight years of starting to act out this new philosophy of care, we were delighted to have won two national awards for the way we look after our clients: the first was a *Daily Telegraph* customer-care award (we were the first professional business of any kind to win it); the second was the Tolley Butterworth award for the best small to medium-sized tax practice, which we won on the strength of our customer-focused approach.

However, it was not until I went on an Accountants' Bootcamp in 1998, four years after my wife and I had stayed at the Savoy, that I began to understand what we had to do to make our ambition to emulate the hotel's customer-care credo a reality. The influence of the Bootcamp – an innovative training programme based in Australia that helps accountants build better practices – was remarkable. Without it we would never have dreamed of entering our practice for a national award based on customer care, let alone winning one.

*

The origin of this book

This book is based on the course notes that accompanied two lectures that I gave on the benefits of value pricing, fixed fees and upfront billing in 2001. The first was given at Oxford University's St Hugh's College at the annual conference of the Tax Faculty of the Institute of Chartered Accountants of England & Wales (ICAEW). While there I raised a salute to St Hugh of Lincoln, the saint to whom that splendid college is dedicated.

I did so for two reasons: firstly, St Hugh happens to be my patron saint and one I believe to have been a kind and wonderful man, and who offers a splendid example of how to live a happy and fulfilling life; secondly, I have a strong hunch that St Hugh would very much approve of the message contained in this volume. Again arranged by the Tax Faculty, the second talk was a lunchtime lecture given at the Chartered Accountants' Hall in Moorgate in London.

Both these lectures came out of an invitation by the then secretary to the Tax Faculty, Chris Peel, to take one of the vacant slots in the annual conference programme. As I explained to Chris when we first discussed the matter, while I am a very enthusiastic apostle of value pricing, I have to confess that I am not necessarily an expert. But as there seems to be nobody else who is prepared to shout about the enormous benefits of this important philosophy to the profession of accountancy, then I willingly step forward to do so.

This philosophy amounts to a wholly new approach to the way in which we serve our clients. While this new thinking applies to everything a professional accountant (or professional *anything*) does, this book focuses on one particular service that we accountants provide: the tax return service, and how we switched to charging a fixed fee for it, as well as billing upfront. However, don't worry if you are a professional who doesn't provide a tax return service because the thinking behind the changes we made in our firm can offer significant benefits if you apply it to your business.

Regardless of what area of practice it is applied to, the principle of upfront billing will
- substantially increase your fees
- allow you to collect the money more quickly
- enable you to build a better relationship with your clients
- cut out masses of time-wasting administrative guff
- help you give your employees more freedom, and more happiness

The last benefit is particularly significant: improving the bottom line is obviously extremely attractive, but the most rewarding aspect of the New Approach is that it allows you to put fulfilling people's needs at the heart of the way you run your business, and to make that focus productive for you, your employees *and* your clients.

At the start of my both of the lectures I have described I said that I felt sure that St Hugh of Lincoln would approve of my message. The reason I was confident of this is that this message (one given a lot of topspin by the Accountants' Bootcamp) is nothing less than an embodiment of the second great commandment of 'Love thy neighbour as thyself'.

*

A note on the Help Sheets

As you read this book I hope that you will begin to agree that we simply have to find a better way of billing than one based on timesheets. But, while you may agree with my suggestions, you may also wonder how you can apply this new approach – how the switch to value pricing will work in practical terms. The Help Sheets that form the second half of the book – predominantly verbatim copies of the letters we sent out to clients to first announce and then administrate the new billing system – will enable you to see exactly how we adopted fixed fees and upfront billing in our practice. Please feel free to crib from them as much as you want, but, equally, you must develop a system that you feel comfortable with.

The benefits of value pricing

CHAPTER ONE

Why timesheets have to go

1. The Mirror Syndrome

Before I indicate the changes that I think professionals should make to the way they bill their clients, I must first explain where I think we as a profession have been going wrong – how the Old Approach is the thing that has been holding us back; how we have to drop it. Doing so will mean rethinking the way we do a number of things in our offices.

I don't know if you have noticed this but nearly every business I know suffers from one particular drawback. They think they know what their business looks like to their customers, and that is all there is to it. But in fact nearly every single business out there does not know very much, if anything, about what people in the outside world think about them.

The role mirrors play in our self-image is a useful analogy here: whether we are male or female, we all look at ourselves in the mirror. We think that the mirror tells us what we look like to the outside world – but it doesn't! One look at a photograph of ourselves shows us that we look very different from what we see in the mirror. Similarly, when we first hear a recorded version of our voice, we tend to say something like 'Help! Do I really sound like that? How dreadful!' We are amazed and some-times embarrassed when we occasionally glimpse ourselves as the world sees us, when we realise that the singular view we have of ourselves isn't shared by others. We think we know our own reality, but I'm afraid we don't. None of us do.

And it is the same with our businesses – they too suffer from the Mirror Syndrome.

Let me give you a classic example of how all businesses (including accountancy practices) suffer from the Mirror Syndrome, one we constantly see evidence of and which glaringly shows how we have one view of our business and the world a completely different one.

How many times have our clients said to us 'I tried newspaper advertising but it didn't work'? They designed the advert and spent a lot of money. It looked OK and it was well-placed on the page. But there was no response. They thought the advert looked terrific. They just loved seeing how wonderful it looked. All that time and money had obviously been well spent. But nobody took a blind bit of notice.

In case you have not worked out why their customers weren't reacting as these firms had hoped, let me ask you: When you pick up a newspaper, why do you do so? I'll tell you what I am planning to read when I pick up a newspaper: the front page, possibly a leader, a short letter, the sports page and maybe the crossword. I do not pick up a newspaper to read the adverts. Some people do but not many. So, when our hoped-for new clients pick up the newspaper with our advert in it, they are just not interested in our, your or anybody else's adverts. It's simply not what they are after when they read a newspaper.

This is the stark reality of the Mirror Syndrome. With our newspaper advert we think we are presenting our business in a way that the world will 'just love'. And no doubt we are presenting our business in a very professional way. We think this is the best way to pitch our advert, given the way the world views our business – that it will be impressed by our advertisement.

But 99.9 per cent of the people reading the newspaper couldn't care less about us and our advertisement! They are simply concerned with what is on their mind at the time and, when they are reading a newspaper, adverts are not what they want to read. If they are looking for a new accountant then they *might* spot your ad, and they *might* phone you up. But the chances of this happening, as we all know, are very slim indeed. Most of those adverts are a waste of money.

I won't dwell on advertising any longer other than to say that, from my own experience, the most productive way to advertise your business is a spot in the *Yellow Pages*. When we pick up a copy of the *Yellow Pages* we are doing so with the sole intention of wanting to find a plumber, accountant or whatever. So, in my view, it is best to spend your advertising budget getting a good *Yellow Pages* advert, using white and other colours to make it stand out – that has certainly worked well for us. I think that most other advertising for our services is a waste of money.

So, to conclude, most adverts do not speak to the way the world views us or the way the world *wants* to view us – they tend to focus on what we want to tell customers rather than what customers actually need from us. The world only views us from its own perspective of 'What can that firm do for *me*? Will they care about *me*? I don't care about *them* and their smart and expensive advert. I want someone to help *me*.'

While we think everyone out there is interested in us and thinks as well of us as we do of ourselves, this is just not the case. People are far too interested in their own selves and cares. Just think of the last time you read a newspaper. Were you really turned on by any of the advertisements you spotted? It is very unlikely that you were.

2. A dose of reality

So to run a truly effective business, we need get a frightening dose of reality and find out how the world looks on us. But how do we find this out?

We go and ask people.

We get our clients to come in and tell us exactly what they think of us. Yes, it is a nerve-wracking experience, but it is well worth it. It was thanks to the Accountants' Bootcamp and the Client Advisory Board they ran for us that we learned what our clients thought of the way we look after them. The Bootcamp invited a number of our clients to attend a meeting, then asked them what they thought of our business, giving us an audio tape of their responses.

So how did it go? In fact it went very well. However, one of the things we found out – and I suspect every accounting and tax practice would find that this applies to them – is that our clients didn't like the way we billed them (Mark Lee says, in the Foreword, that people who respond to his online blog are always telling him this, too). It wasn't the *amount* of the bill, but the fact that the bill remained an unknown quantity for so long.

Our clients complained about 'lack of clarity' in the way we billed. This perceived lack of clarity was not due to lack of narrative – the bill listed all the work we'd done. (Clients never read all that terrible detail anyway – if anything all the verbiage only adds to their unwillingness to pay.) No, what that phrase related to was that clients knew neither what their bill was going to amount to (neither did we until we had added up the hours), nor when it was going to arrive.

Now this gripe came as no surprise to us – clients had often fought us about bills. But when this happened before we had always thought that the client was the one in the wrong. This false assumption that we were right meant that we had never bothered to articulate the problem – or to see if it could be resolved.

The way we used to think was as follows: we had done the work, we had reduced the work-in-progress to a sum that we felt the client would accept, and they should understand that we had every right to expect to be paid the sum on the invoice. We thought we were giving the client a great deal – and, looked at this way, we were right.

But this is the Old Approach in practice and it's wrong.

It is non-thinking.

It must stop.

Thinking this way is to look at our service through our eyes, the eyes we were trained to use. And yet it is not only the wrong way to think, it is immature and out of date.

If you are with me so far, you will already know what I am going to say next. To solve this problem we simply must start looking at our business through the eyes of our clients.

This is terribly easy to do, yet we never do it.

Why is it easy? It is easy because we ourselves are clients. We know how we like to be treated when we are being served by other businesses. I like the way the Savoy does what it does, and you too will have your own favourite suppliers. All we have to do is to apply the philosophy that the best businesses put into practice to the way we run our own businesses.

The thing that I think all professionals should focus on as a means of starting to make a positive shift in the way they bill clients is timesheets. When it comes to billing, have you ever thought how idiotic the method based on timesheets is?

I'll come to why it is so idiotic in more detail in a moment, but before I do, consider this: when any of us buys anything, we don't remove it from the shop without paying for it and without asking the price, then wait for three months for a bill to arrive, not knowing how much it is going to be.

Everything in the world we move about in outside our offices has a price on it. We pay for just about everything before we gain any advantage from it, and we decide to buy on the principle of 'Yes, that seems to be a fair price for the benefit I am going to get from buying it.'

We don't ask the chemist how long it took to make the toothbrush we are thinking of buying. We don't challenge the car salesman on the basis that the men in the factory should have wasted less time in building the vehicle and that we are going to knock off a couple of thousand pounds for coffee and loo breaks.

If we try to get the price of a car reduced it is only on the basis that we are a regular customer and think we should get ten per cent off for loyalty, or because it's got a dent in the wing, or that you should get a special deal because you are offering cash. In everyday circumstances, the price you pay is based on the *value* you perceive you are going to get out of the car, not on the time it took a team of men or women to build it.

Waiting until you have finished the work to send clients their bill totally ignores this link between cost and perceived value – which is a wasted opportunity. And what is the thing that is yoking us to an approach that is so wasteful? The use of the timesheet.

3. Let's stop watching the clock

When we fill out a timesheet, we tend to write down a pack of lies. Or if they are not straight lies then the entries contain a great deal of invention. Let's face facts: we make up a very great deal of what we put on our timesheets.

If you don't accept this accusation, then let me put something to you. For the last hour you have been working on client A's affairs but, during that time, not only did Client B telephone you to ask if he has to pay his latest tax demand straight away, but your fellow partner also called in to ask you if you saw that great programme last night on TV – and you went to the loo.

Now you may have a policy of not charging less than ¼ hour for any work you do for a client, and if you follow this policy you will end up charging 1 ¼ hours for just one hour's work – 1 hour to client A and ¼ hour to client B. But in fact you worked for less than an hour, if you take account of the loo break; yet you charged your clients 1 ¼ hours. This is wrong. The clients know we do this and they hate us for it.

But it is worse than this (or at least it tends to be worse than this): what about the time we spend correcting our own mistakes? If our bills are based on the time we spend working for a client, then the more mistakes we make, the more the client has to pay. That has to be an iniquitous method of charging – there is no other word for it. And, if you doubt my word, would you like being charged for the time the plumber who is installing a new bathroom for you takes to correct the things he shouldn't have got wrong in the first place? Of course not.

Bills based on time records are an absolute no-no. This method really has to stop.

Listen to what outspoken landowner Francis Fulford has to say about us accountants in his book *Bearing Up: The Long View*. He refers to us as 'symbiotic parasites' – hardly a compliment, and then later as 'these dregs of humanity', going on to offer our clients a number of tips that include this one: 'Buy yourself one of those chess clocks, the ones which only start ticking when you press the button, and then stop when you press it again – never attend a meeting without one. Place it ostentatiously on the desk… and only start it when they stop exchanging pleasantries.' Fulford is far from being the only client who feels like this about time recording.

In case there is a reader who truly gazes at their watch every five, six, ten, 12 or 15 minutes and then pulls over the timesheet to write down exactly how they have just spent every moment of that last period, well, may I say 'Get a life!' I have even heard of a firm that charges for every *three* minutes of time spent – I ask you! I'm sorry if that's harsh but it is not only me that regards this kind of practice as being very un-grown up: if you ask your clients they will, almost to a man or woman, agree with both Francis Fulford and myself.

4. Why timesheets are a bad thing for business

As I've said, clients *hate* us recording the time we spend on their affairs. And this is because, by billing them this way, we always force them to ask (if not out loud): 'Couldn't you have done it more quickly?' They also hate it partly because, again as I've said, they never know what the bill is going to be (any more than we do), but also because they know full well that the longer we take – basically, the more incompetent and inefficient we are at preparing their tax return – the more they have to pay. They resent this system because it is so unfair to them: they take all the risk (because they don't know what the final charge will be) and we 'professionals' take none. Beyond damaging our relationship with our clients, there are other good reasons why timesheets are a no-no.

One is that we accountants also hate them. When it comes to filling in our timesheets (if we fill them in at all) most of us do it at the end of the day and therefore end up inventing the way we have spent our time. And yet these lies are the basis on which we calculate the bills we send to our clients. I am staggered when I think of it.

In case you are not yet convinced, here is a list of other very practical reasons why timesheets have to go:
- They take time to fill in.
- They are a real chore. A bore. A job we so often find we haven't done and have to do at the end of a long day, when we are already running late. And the resentment we feel as we spend time filling them in only increases the amount of fiction they contain.
- The details (or in many instances, lies) then have to be transferred to work-in-progress (WIP) sheets. These WIP sheets are then used

to make up the bills – except we hardly ever base them on the WIP totals. We usually reduce the figure to a sum we think the client will accept. So what was the point of writing it all down in the first place? (I mean what *was* the point?!) We could have reached the figure of an appropriate fee so much more quickly if we hadn't spent all that time completing timesheets.

- We have to spend more time writing out not only what work detailed on the WIP sheets we have billed for, but also what work we have written off. We then spend yet more time slogging over WIP reports and doing the billings each month.
- We spend hundreds of pounds on computer programs (I call this not 'time-recording' but 'lie-recording' software) designed to record all this information, as well as on the reams and reams of paper that the WIP sheets get printed on.
- We also spend quite a sum on the storage space in which these files are kept. (I once looked at the space taken up by the accounting paperwork we were filing for a particular year and was amazed to discover that timesheets took up 25 per cent of its volume.)

As accountant and business theorist Ron Baker has pointed out, it is in communist countries that you find economies that are based on hours worked, whereas capitalist markets are based on value pricing. So, if you charge your clients by the hour, you have far more in common with communism than capitalism. Isn't that a remarkable observation by this expert on the subject of value pricing?

As we are embarked on this tirade against timesheets, you might care to think of the following point: many if not most businesses that use timesheets as the method of billing their customers will regard themselves, or at least the partners in their firms, as being self-employed. Indeed their businesses will probably be registered with HM Revenue and Customs as such. I think that, for those firms using timesheets, this registration needs questioning. After all, the designation 'self-employment' implies that the proprietor of such a business works for himself. But, is this true in the case of accountants who are working using timesheets? If you look in the dictionary you will find that an 'employee' is someone employed for wages. If you then look at the definition of wages, wages are sums paid to a worker for the hours, days, etc. that he is at the employer's disposal.

You will be not surprised to learn that, in my view, if the money that this businessman receives is based on the *hours* he works for his clients, he clearly is not working for himself – he is not *self*-employed after all but is actually and by definition working for and employed *by* his *clients*. The client is therefore the employer.

Might not HM Revenue & Customs have a reason for looking more closely at this relationship and charging such clients with failure to operate PAYE properly in connection with the payments they make to their accountant/employee? Such a development would really make our clients really happy, wouldn't it!

Now, in case you have yet to be convinced by my arguments, let us discuss how this iniquitous system of billing for tax returns based on timesheets also leads to all sorts of procedural problems.

5. 'I thought I'd paid for that already'
The way we at HM Williams used to bill for our tax returns was as follows. Once we had prepared the tax return we would look at the WIP sheet at the start of the following month, work out a fee, prepare the bill and send it to the client.

Now you may say, so far so good. But what about the additional time spent on client's tax affairs after the return had been filed?
- The time we spent dealing with the letter we received six weeks later from the Revenue?
- The time we took chasing up the client's tax refund?
- The time we spent giving advice on pension payments?
- Etc., etc., etc...

This time would always be spent and then entered on the WIP records. But the question was *when* should we bill for this additional time? If we sent an extra bill in March, six months after preparing the tax return, even if it was only for £15, what would the client say? Most likely, 'I thought I'd paid for that last year!' And if he was too nice to actually say this, he would still be thinking it.

So did we shrug our shoulders and write it off? We sometimes had to.

Billing based on records of time spent is not only, as I've already emphasised, unfair to the client because they never know what the final fee is going to be, but it is also unfair to accountants because the system always short-changes us, twice: once when we reduce the sum on the bill before we prepare the invoice and again later when we felt that we couldn't bill for the extra hours.

There has to be a better way!

Before I come to that better way, let's look at some of the things we have been trained to do but which show all too clearly to our clients that we use an old, unfriendly approach.

6. Spotting the Old Approach in action

Now you must forgive me if I am veering too far from the world of tax but I think it is worth exploring how you spot a business that is steeped in the Old Approach. For those who do not understand what I am getting at yet with the terms 'Old Approach' and 'New Approach' (and this is a big subject – it took me a few days for it to begin to sink in), it might be useful to point to some of the more explicit signs of whether a business is run according to one or the other modes of thinking.

Notices and signs
Old Approach professionals word their public notices with wording such as 'Keep off the grass' and 'We accept no responsibility for your property'; New Approach professionals post signs that say 'Welcome' and 'We look forward to welcoming you as a client'.

Terms of Engagement
Old Approach professionals use acres of small print to protect them-selves; New Approach professionals simply say how much they are going to do for their customers – they keep their terms as short and friendly as possible.

Who comes first?
Old Approach professionals look after themselves first; New Approach professionals look after their customers first.

What comes first?
Old Approach professionals put profit first; New Approach professionals put customer care first.

My observation is that those people who apply New Approach thinking in the way they run their business:
- Enjoy more fun at work
- Enjoy a better quality of life
- Enjoy better (much better) relationships with their clients
- Make more money

So, ample proof that the Old Approach *has* to go.

Most of us were brought up and trained in the world of the Old Approach. In my view this is a grave handicap. We have come to accept that hourly billing is the only way to bill and we have never thought to question it.

Indeed I would go further. I think it is because of the way we prepare our bills that accountants have, for generations, received a mocking press. Indeed many of us, from time to time, are ashamed and embarrassed to admit that we are accountants – we know that our profession has its critics.

I remember in 1995 attending a meeting at which a senior member of a board of governors, and a man who (like Francis Fulford) hated professional advisers, was in the chair. It was a very hot day. So this man said that everyone, with the exception of the professional advisers, could remove their ties. Now why did he hold us in such disesteem? I think it was because of (what he regarded as) the sly and secretive way that we bill. He resented the way we appear to think we can put whatever we want on our bills and demand payment. I think his behaviour was discourteous but have to admit that the reason for his sneering at us was understandable.

So, the Old Approach is rotten.

It is selfish.

It breeds resentment among our clients.

It is immature.

It is not 'living in the real world'.

7. Bring on the dustbin

When I gave the two lectures in 2001, I used a dustbin as a visual prop to reinforce the point about the huge volume of administrative guff this timesheet-based system creates. In this bin I – with great relish – threw:

- Lever-arch files full of timesheets
- The discs for time-recording software
- The manuals for this software
- Work-in-Progress Records
- Work-in-Progress Write-outs
- Work-in-Progress Write-offs

So far I have been negative, tearing down the past. It's now time to be positive and show you how in practical terms to make the shift away from relying on timesheets.

CHAPTER TWO

Making the switch

1. Announcing the switch to our clients

I am going to start this chapter by explaining the procedure we at
HM Williams adopted to make the switch to a billing system based on
value pricing, an aspect of which was asking for payment upfront.

Now you may ask: didn't the clients resist like mad? You may be
surprised at the answer. Firstly, we sent our clients not one but two
warning letters, openly and clearly explaining the new system and why
we were switching to it – and also explaining the benefits of this change
to them. (Copies of these letters are in the Help Sheets section.)

What we were warning our clients of was that, on the 1st of May,
they would be sent an invoice billing in advance for an all-inclusive tax
return service for the next 12 months. The bill had to be paid by the end
of May, or a standing order had to be set up by then, and from that point
on we would guarantee to do everything necessary in relation to their
tax affairs for that 12-month period – and that there would be no further
charges. In our case, that meant 250 warning notices going out in the
middle of March, and then another set at the very start of the tax year.

Would you like to guess how many letters of complaint or objection
we received? What would you expect?

Nobody, but nobody told us they objected to having to pay upfront.
I promise that this is gospel truth.

So, if you would like to make the switch to value pricing in your business, when is the best time to do so? I think the answer has to be that, if
you are reading this in (say) the first six months of a new tax year, that
now may not be the best time to introduce such a new concept in billing.
You may want to leave it and put it into effect early in the next tax year.
However, if you think it is the right time for you, regardless of the time

left in the tax year, then go for it. Others have started this process in the latter half of the tax year, and the system has worked.

2. Time to catch up

Although I've made the point previously, it really is worth emphasising again how ridiculous it is that by still basing our bills on timesheets the majority of us are so out of step with the rest of the world. Nearly every other business out there prices its goods and services upfront and it expects to be paid upfront. To underline the fact that nearly everyone else has accepted this as common-sense logic, it's worth listing a few more examples:

- The Institute of Chartered Accountants asks us for our subscriptions upfront.
- The Institute's Tax Faculty wanted payment for a place at its spring conference *before* the delegates arrived.
- The railway company asks you for your money *before* you board the train.
- The garage asks you for the money for the petrol *before* you restart the engine and drive away.
- Your newspaper has to be paid for *before* you read it.
- Your shopping has to be paid for at the checkout *before* you leave and *well before* you unwrap it at home and start to consume it.
- School fees have to be paid for *before* term starts.
- We are forever seeing the phrase 'Money-back guarantee' on offers in advertisements, etc. What does it imply? That you pay *before* you get the product. Indeed it is a given that you will have no objection whatever to being asked to part with your cash before you even get hold of and test the product. Why else would a company be offering you your money back if you hadn't already paid for the product upfront?

Do you or anybody you know ever moan about paying upfront? Of course not. This is how the real world operates.

Indeed, running the service in this way is a little like the RAC subscription, which has to be paid for on the 1st of January. The big difference here of course is that if you pay our 'sub' we *guarantee* to do something for you – over the course of a year the RAC may do nothing for a customer. This is yet another example of the customer paying in advance for a service.

We have to realise that paying upfront is the way that 99 per cent of people not only do business but *expect* to do business. It's about time we accountants adopted a practice that is so universal.

The fact upfront billing is such a norm in the world beyond accountants' offices is the reason why our clients did not object to our switching to it. It is why your clients won't object either.

To conclude this point: there is nothing immoral or greedy about asking to be paid upfront. It is the only way for most businesses to do business. Indeed I would argue that it is in fact immoral *not* to be asked to be paid upfront.

3. The crunch – clients receive their bills

How did our 250 clients react when their pre-pay bills actually arrived?

In the previous year our tax return work had earned us around £50,000. The 250 invoices we sent out on the 1st of May totalled about £67,000 – so we had built in an increase of over 30 per cent on the previous year's figure.

In response to the letters we had calls from 15 of our clients – all people who had not bothered to read either of our two warning letters. Clients were not upset, but (as is their absolute right) they wanted to chat about the change.

The net result of all this? We lost ten clients as a result of the switch. The total fees that those people accounted for were about £2,000. They were all what one would call the 'smaller' clients. And, crucially, they went more because of the increase in fees than because we were asking them to pay for our service upfront. It may be that we lost a few because the bill was upfront. I personally think it was none.

The figures tell the story. We had lost a few clients, yes, but we had added a net 30 per cent to our bottom line on our tax return service.

And what about the longer term? Although we had made the switch to upfront billing, we did not stop filling out timesheets. At the end of the year, when I did the work-in-progress sums for our tax return service, there was a credit of £2,200. In other words, overall, we had just won on the deal. However, the next year we lost £1,800 on the tax return service.

Having seen how the figures balanced out over those two years, we decided to ditch all time recording – no one in our office has filled out a timesheet for this purpose since.

So that was how we made the switch – if you want to follow our example, you can find details of how we did it in the Help Sheets section.

CHAPTER THREE

Value pricing: why it's good for clients

1. The benefits of fixed fees and upfront billing

Everything is clear
The client knows what the fee is going to be before we start to work on his affairs (and at last we are giving him the courtesy he is owed for bringing us the work).

This means that if the client thinks the fee is too high, he now has a clear and fair choice. He can either ask us whether it could be reduced, possibly in return for a reduced level of service. Or he can take his business elsewhere. Obviously, we hope this will not happen but if it should happen there is, using the upfront billing system, the new and significant advantage for both sides that neither party hurts if we part company.

The client does not hurt because he does not have to part with any cash for a service he didn't think was good value; and the accountant does not hurt because no work has been done for which he hasn't been paid. They can part company friends.

There need never be a row about fees again!

No nasty surprises
The client does not get any surprise bills. At least, if one *is* a surprise, he has an excuse for walking away from it without paying.

Anxiety-free access
Having agreed to the fee by paying the bill, the client can then contact or visit you at any time without harbouring that age-old worry that goes with an Old Approach relationship with an accountant: 'What's this costing me?' The answer is 'Nothing! It's all been paid for upfront.'

Sense of control

This new situation gives the client the feeling that he or she is in the driving seat on fees. This sense of control is something that timesheets never ever give them.

More goodwill

The new clarity in the way clients are billed greatly improves their relationship with their accountant. Clients are nicer to us – and this is because we are being more open with them. And this means more recommendations by them to their friends. Here is what a client wrote to me on this very subject:

> I wanted to write and tell you how much I appreciate your new way of charging a flat fee for the work you do over my tax return. Whereas before I always thought twice before ringing to ask questions, now I feel that you will welcome them, however trivial they are. I am also very grateful to know that, if the Revenue mounts an inspection, you will deal with it for me.
>
> Your new system has turned what was a strictly professional and impersonal relationship into a friendship which I value.

In short, this client now trusts us more (far more) – as do all our other clients.

Less small print

If you look at the way we word our invoice for our tax return service (copy enclosed in the Help Sheets section), you will see we have done away with the need for separate terms of engagement. We now use just a simple set of conditions that are printed on the invoice itself.

And as long as the client pays us on time and sends his papers to us on time, the scenario over the remainder of the tax year is a one-way process of benefits flowing towards the client. In my view, you won't need any small print. Whether or not clients read it, small print only breeds resentment.

More efficient service
Receiving a fixed fee in advance focuses the mind wonderfully, meaning we probably do the work more quickly – which of courses benefits the client.

Far less risk
By billing upfront and thereby taking full responsibility for the time involved in processing our clients' tax affairs for a full year, we remove all the risk in the relationship for the client – there is now no chance that they will get billed more than they anticipated, or have to pay unfairly for slices of time that were not in reality spent on their affairs. It is our profession's hitherto sly behaviour, this secrecy about fees and time spent, that led the discourteous chairman of that hot meeting in 1995 to hold us in such low regard. As I said, he had a point. And, of course, it is the fact that we, and not our clients, now take the risk – the risk of not getting paid for all the work you have done. This is a significant part of the justification for the increase in fees that I strongly recommend you implement.

2. The comfort of a guarantee
So, the client receives many benefits from this new system – but there is one vital aspect to this whole new approach: it offers clients complete peace of mind. What this means is that, in return for having to make a payment upfront, the client gets a guarantee, a guarantee that our tax return service will be stress-free and that if it isn't (and they are the only judge in the matter) that they can simply ask for their money back.

We remove stress from the equation by telling a client when we start to work for them that we are making them a number of promises (promises that remain active as long as a client both pays the fee and sends their papers to us on time):
- We will process their tax return and then deal with all other matters relating to their tax affairs over the course of the year at no extra cost, despite the fact we have no way of knowing exactly how many brown envelopes are going to arrive for them during that time.
- We will tell them that their return has been safely lodged, so they can rest assured that everything has been dealt with on time.
- We will pay any automatic penalties, not them.
- They can ring us up at any time in connection with their tax affairs and it won't cost them a penny.
- When they write to us they can send their papers using Freepost.

- They can request one of our free in-house tax return organisers – we call them Taxafiles.
- They can pay either by credit card or standing order.
- If our work doesn't delight them that they can ask for their money back.

Now you may be saying to yourself 'Aren't we already providing these benefits and guarantees?' The answer may well be that you may be providing them but the chances are that you haven't *told* the clients that you are. In far too many cases the guarantees are hidden by never being declared, and are only revealed when a client starts to moan and has to dig them out for himself. And when a client does this, such guarantees are usually given somewhat grudgingly and received by the client somewhat ungratefully – using guarantees in this way is not good practice.

To get the full benefit from guarantees you have to say to clients at the first meeting: 'By the way, if you are not happy with our service, with us it's simple – you don't pay, or you ask for and get a full refund. You are the only judge on our level of service, and we will never quibble.' That sort of approach really impresses clients and would-be clients.

Now you may be saying 'But surely the clients will abuse this sort of gold-plated guarantee?' In reply I would say that in my experience the benefits arising from the increase in trust that this guarantee creates between clients and their advisers far outweighs the negatives caused by the minuscule number of small-minded clients who want to take you for a ride. And if a client does take you for a ride, you simply get rid of them.

Let me mention one final thing about guarantees: as a practice we are always trying to find ways of increasing the number of our promises. This is part of the fun of running a practice based on the New Approach. Professionals who do so are constantly trying to improve the way they look after their clients.

3. One exception to the rule on tax services
The only exception we make to billing upfront for our tax return service is when an unforeseen capital-gains tax matter takes a disproportionate amount of time to resolve. In this case we reserve the right to charge extra but only if we fix that extra sum in advance and agree with the client that this extra sum is appropriate. If the client disagrees we don't raise the extra fee note.

4. Expanding the New Approach

As a result of the Client Advisory Board that the Accountants' Bootcamp ran for us, we could see that *everything* we do should be on the basis of 'upfrontness'. So each April we now write to all of our clients telling them what our fees are going to be for *all* of our services (you will find copies of the relevant paperwork in the Help Sheets section).

When we can, we also try to bill upfront, too. However, asking for the money in advance of the work is not appropriate for everything – not all the work we do is spread over a year-long period, as with the tax return service. (The tax return service is a bit different to everything else in this respect – and this is why I maintain that it should *always* be billed for upfront.) As we know, accounts work, auditing, etc. tends to take place over a discrete period, which is normally a matter of just a few weeks. The rest of the time the paperwork is simply gathering dust. With this in mind, there is no need to bill for these types of services upfront on the 1st of May. However, should the client wish to pay us upfront for their accounts, etc., we set up a standing order so that they can spread the payments evenly over a year. This helps them budget. And it helps us, too. Another case of 'win-win'.

5. Clients have been waiting for upfront billing

It is worth saying that even before we switched everyone who used our tax service to upfront billing, a lot of our clients were already asking us if we could bill them in this way. So this major switch in our billing pattern was heralded by the requests of people *outside* of our business.

Indeed, when I mention the fact that our tax return fees are billed upfront to clients who don't yet know us, I frequently find they say that this suits them better than the old timesheet method.

6. Other professional's clients like upfront billing

Professionals in many areas have already made the switch – and their clients appreciate them practising the New Approach. I myself fairly recently enjoyed the benefits of a professional shouldering the risk in our financial relationship.

In June 2001 (the day of the general election, to be exact) I had a cataract removed from my right eye. I was in no hurry to get this done and so I had the operation on the NHS. Had I gone private this procedure would have cost me £1,800.

The operation normally lasts between 15 and 20 minutes, or, in the parlance of the accountant, costs £100 per minute.

However in my case, there were complications. This meant that my operation in fact lasted over an hour – it was, the surgeon said, '*Guinness Book of Records* stuff'. As I got up off the operating table I asked the surgeon whether, had I gone private, the charge for my unusually protracted operation would have been increased – by my reckoning, using the timesheets principle, it might have cost 60 minutes at £100, meaning a total fee of £6,000. But, no, I was told that the operation is fixed price.

I then told the surgeon about the lectures I had been giving on this subject and he said 'Good for you – could you address the solicitors as well?!'

So you see, there can be no argument – none at all!

Upfront billing *has* to be right.

CHAPTER FOUR

Value pricing: why it's good for firms

1. The benefits of upfront billing

i. Improved client relations. It may take a little time for the clients to accept and adopt the change, but, once it has bedded in, they will, as I suggested in the previous chapter, both like and trust you more.

ii. Cash flow is improved – the money comes in far sooner.

iii. By offering a 12-month-long service you are offering a better service, one that is more valuable than just filling in the tax return. This gives you a golden opportunity to put your fees up. As I have said, this is what we did. You must do the same, particularly because you are now taking the financial risk you had previously left on your clients' shoulders – this is a real value-added extra feature of your new service. So, charge more and you will find that not only does the cash come in faster but more of it comes in.

iv. Budgeting becomes easier because you have a much better fix on what your total fees are going to be for a year.

v. As I've described in previous chapters, all the tedious administration in the form of timesheets and WIP simply disappears. *Disparut*!

vi. Billing is so much quicker and simpler. Indeed you as a partner never (well, more or less never) need generate a bill again. The sum for all your services has been advised to the clients in April each year, and therefore agreed in advance. So, when it comes to billing, all the employee (not the partner) has to do is look up the figure, prepare the bill at the appropriate time and send it off.

Isn't this so much easier than pouring over time sheets, WIP reports and agonising over how much to charge?

2. A very new benefit

There is one more, very important additional advantage of upfront billing, which has only emerged as a result of last year's change in the accounting rules.

Upfront billing and quoting upfront for all work fits in very neatly with the requirements of revenue recognition laid down by UITF Abstract 40 (UITF40). In simple terms, what this means is that, in the case of accounting periods ending after 22 June 2005, where work on a particular contract has been partially completed at the end of the accounting year, the proportion of work completed but not billed at that date should be valued at selling price and no longer at the lower of cost or net realisable value. Whether we like it or not, this is how we now have to value what we will probably still call 'work in progress', even if it is now more properly termed 'accrued income'.

So under the new upfront system we work out this sum by reference to the bill we send to the client and *not* the costs in our time records. With timesheets you have to look at the costs incurred to date and then multiply that sum by a suitable proportion to estimate the revenue you believe you have earned on this contract, even though you are a long way from sending out a bill. But it will be a hit and miss affair because you don't know what you will finally bill.

If you use upfront billing, where you have already billed for the work there will be no need to change your accounting system to cater for the demands of UITF40. You already comply with the rules as you will have a sum of 'fees billed in advance'.

In addition, if there is work you are doing that you are not billing upfront, you will know what the bill will amount to because you will have quoted for it upfront, so you simply have to scale that sum down by the proportion of work that remains to be done to get the job to completion.

So, a life without timesheets is tailor-made for coping with UITF40. Once again the upfront system wins hands down.

3. Fixing the right price

Before getting started with the new system, you need to set the right fee. The question is how to set a fee for the tax return service that both makes a profit and is fair to the client, now that you may no longer enjoy the apparent safety net of WIP reports?

The answer has to be a price that you feel is correct (and some of us might say that we are, after all, accountants, and so of all people ought to know how to work out such a sum).

But you can get a few pointers. You can ask your next new client what their budget for their tax return service is. If you go into an estate agents looking to buy a house, or a garage showroom for a new car, one of the very first questions you will be asked is 'How much were you looking to spend?' Why don't we ask our clients this?

You can also ask other accountants. At HM Williams we belong to Heads Together, a small of group of accountancy firms that shares its figures each year. Although our fee levels for are not very clearly broken down by service on our own Inter-Firm Comparative Report Sheet, from looking at it we can get a pretty good idea of whether we are charging enough.

Lastly, you could always ask the Institute of Chartered Accountants for guidance.

But, in principle, fixing the right price is what being in business is all about. If we are to be worthy accountants, it's a nettle we simply have to grasp.

But in case you are at risk of fixing the price too low, I do urge you to think big when it comes to selling the value you give. If your fees are too low, your reward will be low – the world values you at the level you charge. I know of one first-rate tax adviser who used to charge all his clients so little that most people didn't take him seriously. I was always telling him to put his fees up. I am glad to say that when it comes to the work he now does for my clients, he has listened and his fees have leapt up by 200 per cent – and we are giving him a lot more work than we were when his fees were far too low.

If you want to think of yourself as being the best tax adviser – or anything else – in town, you had better charge top rates. That way you will get the best work and the best rewards. If you are ashamed of asking for a good (and proper) fee, then you will never make any money. Be proud of your service and walk to work with a confident step. This doesn't mean that you have to actually *have* the best tax brain in town – it simply means that you will need to be better at looking after your clients' worries and concerns than your fellow professionals.

As I've already said, if you do decide to switch to value pricing, take it as a golden opportunity to increase your fees by a big percentage – something big enough to get you a proper reward for all your training and hard work. Yes, you will lose some clients but nothing like as many as you might fear, and the ones that go, you will soon discover, were the ones you didn't really like working for anyway.

And, as I again want to emphasise, this increase in fees is entirely justified. There is nothing but *nothing* immoral or sharp-practised about it. This is because, not only are you providing a much better service than those firms that charge by the hour, but, above all, you and not the client, are now taking (and you are now seen to be taking) the risk as far as the cost of the process is concerned. This key aspect alone – this sea change in the level of service that you will be providing – has to be worth a very significant increase in fees over the level charged by those who add up the hours, send a bill and let the client take the risk.

4. Fees for non-tax services

This new philosophy results in significantly higher fees all round – not just for tax returns. You might find it helpful to see how, in detail, this approach can lead to healthy fees for value-added services. Let me give you two examples:

Example 1
At HM Williams we have looked after a lady for nearly 15 years. She has moaned about fees in the past. Her annual tax return service costs her £450 + VAT. (Now, what I am about to relate is not just telling tales – I am not asking for sympathy, but merely setting the scene.)

A few years ago this lady invited me to her birthday party. I think it was four times she came up to me and said to the people I was talking to 'You don't want to talk to Hugh for too long or he'll send you a bill!' Now I would say that, of all firms, HM Williams is really not guilty of such a charge. We both quote and bill upfront.

I think it was because the party was held fairly soon after this client had received her annual bill for our tax return service that she joked this way. But she wasn't being fair because, as I've already explained, we give all clients the chance to walk away from our fees without paying. Nonetheless, this lady kept trying to embarrass me on her big day.

The following January, the same client wrote to me asking about the possibility of saving on inheritance tax. I told her we could probably save her £½ million.

Here's how I quoted for the fee: I said that the process would take six months, and I anticipated that I would need to spend 15 hours a month on it. I said that my charge-out rate was £100 an hour, totalling £9,000 for the hours quoted. I then applied a 20 per cent discount as a cushion in the event that we covered the work more quickly than anticipated. The final quote was therefore £7,200 + VAT. (Now maybe I should have quoted more – if you were to do so I would salute you, but £7,200 was the fee we quoted.)

She replied saying, 'Fine' and thanked me for the discount, sending the cheque a couple of weeks later – and long before we had really started working on the case.

And a few months later, after the exercise had been completed, she sent me an effusive thank you letter for what we had done for her.

The point I am making here is that we got a client to swallow a fee over ten times that of her annual tax return service, to pay upfront and be delighted at the same time. If we had billed her at the end of the process and on an hourly basis I suspect that she would have resisted paying anything over £1,000.

Example 2

The second case concerns a man who we also charge about £400 per year and who is tight about fees. We told him that he could save something like £50,000 in tax if we registered his company under the Enterprise Investment Scheme.

Now we had never done this before and did not know what to charge. I 'phoned a friend' and was told that £750 to £1,000 was what they charged. To me this seemed far too low in view of the huge financial benefit the client would enjoy as a result of our service.

So I wrote to the client along similar lines to those used in example 1 (i.e. so many anticipated hours over so many months, less a 20 per cent discount) and the figure came to £8,640 + VAT. I also mentioned to the client that if we failed to get the registration accepted, we would not charge him a fee. He accepted the £8,640 like a lamb, and he particularly liked what he called the 'No Foal No Fee' guarantee!

The exact wording we used when writing to these two clients about our fees can be seen in the relevant section of the Help Sheets.

5. The advantages for employees

Your employees too will enjoy significant benefits from the switch to upfront billing.

1. They no longer face the chore and bore of filling in timesheets any more.

2. They no longer have to transfer details from the timesheet to the work-in-progress sheets.

3. Neither will they... Here we go again – I won't repeat what I have already said about WIP. Let's just accept that that whole WIP system should be consigned to the dustbin.

4. By not trying to pin your employees down – asking them to account for every moment they have spent each day (and let's face it, are you that much of a tyrant that you need to insist on knowing such trivia?) – you start to treat them as grown-ups. As a result they will feel so much better about you and about their work. Indeed, when we interview for new employees and tell them that we don't fill in timesheets, you can see their eyes light up at the thought.

Before closing this section, let me mention one final point. The switch to upfront billing is particularly important because now that your billing is based on *value* pricing, you will find that when you are working out the amount of the upfront fee and ask your employees 'What do you think is a fair charge in this case?' they will tend to be far more objective than you and usually their suggested fee will be higher than the figure you had in mind.

So, if you are now convinced that timesheets have to go, you can move on to Section II, a collection of Help Sheets that will enable you to employ some or all of the methods that we used when we switched from timesheets to upfront billing. I hope you will find our model useful.

It goes without saying that if you are now one of those people who wishes to ditch the outdated and unfriendly system of billing by the hour, I salute you as you move towards a new *Life without Timesheets.*

Making value pricing work

Applying the principle

What the Help Sheets are for

The rest of this book is made up of Help Sheets – predominantly letter templates that are verbatim copies of those we sent out to clients at different stages of the shift to upfront billing and beyond – that will help you make the switch. But will following their example work for you?

You may be interested to know what happened when another firm used exactly the same procedure as we did to switch to upfront billing. I quote from their thank-you letter:

> As we did not wish to delay it until next year, we adapted it slightly and sent out 80 bills at the beginning of September. So far (9th November) 80 per cent have been paid *without complaint* [my emphasis].
>
> There were three outright refusals. Two refused to pay in advance and could only be retained by an agreement that they could continue on the old basis; and one decided to do his own return in future.
>
> Overall it was a much better outcome than I had been expecting and the improvement to the cash flow and the reduction in internal record-keeping mean that the plan has already more than paid for itself.
>
> We are therefore very pleased with the whole thing and are very grateful to you.

So, independent confirmation from another firm that switching to upfront billing really works.

What each Help Sheet shows you

1. First letter we sent to our clients warning them that we were switching to upfront billing

2. Second letter we sent to our clients warning them that we were switching to upfront billing

3. Annual letter (sent in mid-April) advising clients in advance of their fees for the next year

4. Advance Notice of Fees for the forthcoming year (enclosed with letter described in item 3)

5. The upfront bill

6. Letter thanking the client for supplying tax papers and requesting that they sign and post back their tax return

7. Letter explaining to a doubting client why the tax return fee is now billed upfront

8. Handout for members of the office team to help them if a client should complain about upfront billing

9. Letters illustrating the wording used when telling two clients how we were going to bill them in a 'value added' way for
   Example 1   Inheritance Tax Mitigation
   Example 2   Registering a Company under the Enterprise Investment Scheme

10. Thoughts for members of the office team on dealing with client complaints

11. Letter to a prospective client telling them what their fees will be

12. The pro-forma letter for clients to sign and return in response to a quote from us

13. Spreadsheets that help you control the billing process

First letter we sent to our clients warning them that we were switching to upfront billing

> This warning was sent out as a prominent part of a newsletter that we circulated to all clients six weeks before the bills were to be posted.

Dear

Changes to the way we send out our tax return invoices
From 1 May 1998 we will be adopting a new method of billing for our annual tax return services. On that day we will be issuing invoices for our services for the 1998 tax return (but excluding accounts preparation) to all our clients. These fee notices will be due for payment by 31 May 1998.

The reasons for this change are as follows:
While the bulk of our tax return work involves the preparation of the tax return form itself, there is a great deal of other work that is attended to throughout the year (issuing reminders, correspondence with yourselves, correspondence with the tax office, checking notices of coding, tax demands, telephone calls, etc.) and it is virtually impossible in any case to draw a line, send an invoice and regard the work as completed. One never knows when the next post will mean we have to open the file again and incur more time. So we feel that an annual all-in fee for a complete tax return service would be more appropriate than the present practice of submitting an invoice after the tax return has been completed.

The benefits of this for our clients will be:
- You will know in advance what your annual tax return fee will be. There will be no extras, unless of course you give us extra non-tax return work to attend to, such as accounts preparation.
- You can rest assured that you can telephone or write to us at any time and we will not be 'switching on the fees clock' (in fact we don't do this now but you are forgiven if you think that we do!). We hope this will make us more approachable.
- You can pay over 12 months by standing order, if you prefer.
- If this presents any problems please let us know.

Yours sincerely

HELP SHEET 2

Second letter we sent to our clients – on 1 April – warning them we were switching to upfront billing

Dear

A new tax teturn year begins on 6 April 200x

So that we can serve you best in completing your tax return before the deadline, we are writing to set out the process by which that would be best accomplished. You will want to avoid penalties and interest for late submission of your return, so you will understand that we will need a reasonable amount of time in which to do the work. With that in mind we would like to ask you to submit all of your information to us by *30 June at the latest*.

Many of our clients find that our Taxafile system helps them gather all of the relevant information quickly. If you do not yet have a Taxafile and would like to have one, just call us and we will dispatch it to you with a Freepost return label.

Would you please let us know if you would like a copy of last year's tax return for use as a checklist?

Please note that invoices for our all-inclusive tax return service will be issued on 1 May 200x and are due for payment by 31 May 200x unless you wish to pay by standing order, in which case the standing order must be set up by 31 May.

Pricing for this annual service in this way gives you the advantages of (a) knowing in advance what the fee will be and (b) giving you a comprehensive tax return service that enables you to telephone or write to us at any time in connection with your tax return, but with nothing more to pay. Additionally, you can also pay by standing order or credit card.

If any of this should present any problems please let us know.

Yours sincerely

HELP SHEET 3
Annual letter (send in mid-April) advising clients in advance of their fees for the next year

Dear

Advance notice of our fees for 2007/2008
A number of our clients have asked us to give them advance notice of their fees so that they can complete their budgets and make appropriate decisions. We have therefore decided, wherever possible, to give all our clients this extra service. The details are on the attached sheet.

The fee for your 2007 tax return service (where one is shown) is an all-inclusive fee for 12 months. For instance, you can telephone us as much as you want about any aspect of your tax return, and there is nothing more to pay. This invoice will be raised on 1st May 2007 and will be due for settlement by the end of that month.

Other fees, which are the maximum we will charge for the potential services required, are as shown on the attached sheet and will be raised when the work has been completed. Payment will be due by the end of that month.

Remember also our overriding guarantee – if you are not satisfied with our service (and you are the sole judge) you don't pay.

You need take no action on receipt of this letter. However, if it would help you to pay for our fees by standing order over ten months, please let us know as soon as possible.

Finally, thank you for the business you have brought our way. We are very grateful.

Yours sincerely

HELP SHEET 4
Advance Notice of Fees for the forthcoming year (enclosed with letter shown in Help Sheet 3)

Client Number:

Proposed Fees for	**£ex - VAT**
Tax return service from 6 April 2007 to 5 April 2008 – to be invoiced on 1 May 2007 and payable by 31 May 2007	
Preparation of your accounts for the period to _____	
Audit of your accounts to _____	
Preparing monthly PAYE records for ____ employees (together with preparing related year end PAYE documents, to be billed quarterly) for 2007/2008	
Preparation of your Corporation Tax return for 2007/2008	
Preparation of ____ Management Accounts during the year to _____ _____ × £xxx	
Preparation of ____ dividends & related tax submissions	
Checking your 2008 P35 return Company Secretarial Services for your Company to ____ (including completion of Annual Return)	

continued overleaf

Preparation of Dormant Company Accounts to

_____

Preparation of four VAT returns during the year to

_____

Other Services:

_____

_____

Total

Finally

1. *If you would like to pay by standing order (12 × £ + VAT), please ask us to send you a form. Alternatively, you can pay by credit card.*

2. *Notes: this is not a VAT invoice, nor is it a request for payment.*

HELP SHEET 5
The upfront bill

> Note that the sum payable is mentioned at the *top* of the letter. This way, as the client reads down the page, they keep reading about the benefits of our service. In other words, the last thing the client reads are the *benefits* – not the price.

Invoice No:

Fee for our services in connection with your 2007 tax return
VAT @ 17.5 per cent
Total (due by 31 May 2007)

The way our annual tax return service works is as follows: if you would kindly settle this invoice by 31 May and send us your tax return papers by 30 June 2007, in return we will:

- complete your 2007 tax return and send it to you to review and sign, and then return to us.
- tell you how much tax you will have to pay (when we send you your tax return).
- file your tax return via the internet and let you know as soon as we receive acknowledgement from the Inland Revenue that it has been processed (so you need not even begin to worry about automatic penalties).
- send you a payslip for submitting with your tax cheque, should you require one.
- chase you if you don't get on with this!
- send you a reminder to prepare for the 2008 tax return
- In short, for a one-off payment we will look after all of this for you for 12 months to 30 April 2008

In addition:
- you can correspond with us by Freepost and pay by either credit card or standing order.
- you can enjoy the free use of one of our Taxafiles (your personal tax return organiser).
- you can telephone, write, email or fax us at any stage about your tax return and there are no extra charges. *This is an all-inclusive fee.*

Because the tax return work is handled by team members who we both train and value, in many cases the letter accompanying the tax return will be signed by the person who carried out the work. In other words, we are all at your service.

HELP SHEET 6
Letter thanking the client for supplying tax papers and requesting that they sign and post back their tax return

Dear

Tax return – year ended 5 April 2007
First of all, thank you for sending us your tax return papers. As a result of your help, we can enclose:

1. Your tax return covering your income for the year ended 5 April 2007. I have prepared this myself and Hugh has reviewed the file and approved the return for sending to you. However, as you will remember, under the law the HMRC regard the completion of the tax return as a taxpayer's personal responsibility. Will you therefore please review this return carefully to ensure that we have disclosed all the information properly.

2. Your own bound copy of the tax schedule. Please retain this yourself.

3. An envelope containing your 2007 tax return vouchers. Please retain these until 6 April 2013.

4. A 2008 Taxafile to help you with filing tax vouchers and any other material that relates to next year's tax return. Also, a Freepost label for use next year.

If you are satisfied that the return is both complete and correct, please sign and date the declaration where indicated on page 8 and send the form back to us in the enclosed Freepost envelope. *Please return it to us as soon as possible as there are penalties for late submission.* When we get your return back we intend to submit it to the Inland Revenue by electronic means.
Based on the enclosed tax return, and subject to any amendments that may be necessary after you have checked it, we calculate your overall tax payable on 31 January 2008 to be in accordance with the enclosed tax calculation.
I hope this all makes sense, but do please contact us if you have any queries.

Yours sincerely

Tax Calculation

As a result of submitting this 2007 tax return we believe that you will have income tax to pay as follows:

Payments due

Total tax and Class 4 NIC for 2006/7		£5,000.00
Less:		
Payment on account due 31 January 2007	£2,000.00	
Payment on account due 31 July 2007	£2,000.00	
		(£4,000.00)
Balancing payment due		£1,000.00
Payment on account		£2,500.00
Payment due by 31 January 2008		£3,500.00
Payment on account due by 31 July 2008		£2,500.00

Useful information

The first tax payment of £3,500.00 is due on 31 January 2008. Interest will be charged on any late payment, and possibly a surcharge as well. Could you please, therefore, ensure that the tax reaches the Collector of Taxes in good time, but remember that we are here to help you, so please ask us if you have any queries.

You should receive a statement from the HMRC reminding you of forthcoming payments, together with a paying-in slip. It is recommended that you clearly write your tax reference number (as shown on the paying-in slip) on the back of your cheques. The cheques should be made payable to 'Inland Revenue Only', followed by your tax reference.

If you do not receive a payslip, please contact us and we can supply you with one. This is important because, again under the law, not receiving such a payslip will not be regarded by the HMRC as a reasonable excuse for late payment of tax.

HELP SHEET 7

Letter explaining to a doubting client why the tax return fee is now billed upfront

Dear

Thank you for your letter of 200x.

One of the reasons for sending invoices 'upfront' is so that we can have exchanges like this without hurting. So that when I say 'thank you' I *mean* thank you.

The strange thing is that, only last week we had an enquiry from a new client who wanted to come to us because we charged upfront. That was our selling point.

We have decided to charge upfront for a number of reasons, all of which are in the client's interest. However, in case you are thinking that there is something improper about charging upfront, I think it is true to say that most things in life are paid for before we can enjoy them (school fees, RAC subscriptions, shopping, train fares, etc., etc.), and so, by sending an invoice in advance, we are only doing what most of the rest of the business world does. Incidentally, you last paid for your tax returns last May so a full 12 months has elapsed since we last asked for payment for this service.

However, coming back to the benefits for the client, the main one is it gives you the choice. If you don't like the charge, you don't have to buy and, should we part company, neither of us hurt.

The alternative is for us to continue charging you when we have seen how long it has taken us and the effect of this is that the longer we take (ie. the more inefficient we are) the more you have to pay and we don't think this is fair to you. However, on top of this, the client is left biting his nails worrying about what the fee will be. The fact that we are totally transparent in our charges means none of these worries cross your mind.

The other thing that we guarantee (and what professional guarantees *anything* these days?) is the fact that there will be *nothing* more for you to pay. In other words, no matter how long we take, no matter how many times you ask us about your tax affairs, it has all been paid for. We have had a number of clients telling us how much they like this because, you can now pick up the phone and you can guarantee that we have not started the clock at the same time. You will notice that, in view of all the meetings we had last autumn, we never charged you a bean for them. Indeed, now that we have completed the first year of the new system, and our clients have been able to see that we stuck to our word and did not send out any more invoices, the validity of our claim that it is an all-inclusive service has been proved and appreciated by a number of clients.

On top of this you can pay by standing order over 12 months so that your payments end by the time our work is completed.

Accordingly I hope you can see that we are behaving properly and that we can still be in business. I am returning the invoices.

With best wishes.

Yours ever

Handout for members of the office team to help them if a client should complain about upfront billing

Things to say to clients who ask about the change to upfront billing

1. We started upfront billing in 1998 when, one by one, clients began to ask for it.

2. Putting an upfront price on our services puts the clients in the driving seat over fees, not us. This is because if the client does not like what we are proposing to charge, while we hope that we can come to an agreement, the client is free to go elsewhere and if we should part company, we do so as friends. We part as friends because the client has not paid more than he or she wants, and we have not done work for which we have not been paid. Nobody loses. As one of our professional friends said the other day, 'It is much nicer for the client'.

3. In 1998 a group of clients all said that they wanted it.

4. Billing on an hourly basis is unfair to clients because:
    *   clients don't know what it will cost
    *   the longer we take (the more inefficient we are) the more they pay. This we want to ensure never happens to our clients.

5. We now take the risk, not the client. Hourly billing leaves the risk with the client. Using the old method, the client ran the risk of not knowing what the charge would be. That risk has now been removed.

6. In return for billing upfront we now offer four guarantees:
    *   we pay automatic penalties
    *   the client pays no postage
    *   there will be nothing more to pay, no matter how often the clients bother us about their tax returns – this is an all-inclusive fee
    *   if the client is not delighted, we offer a full refund

7. A client may have the free use of one of our Taxafiles.

8. Everything is paid for upfront these days. From shopping to the car-park fee, from houses to a pint of beer, from newspapers to train fares, from rent to

school fees, from the RAC subscription to council tax, from the car licence to the TV licence, from club subscriptions to pension and insurance premiums. The only businesses that do not see the sense of up-front billing are the professions. However, the more enlightened firms are changing because they can see that it is so much better for the client. We are proud to think that we have been doing this for over two years.

9. When we began to do this, the overwhelming majority of our clients could see the sense of this (how it was better for them) with *very* few exceptions.

10. There is everything to be said for upfront billing, just so long as we give guarantees in return – ie. money back if we fail to deliver.

Letters illustrating the wording used when telling two clients how we were going to bill them in a 'value added' way

Example 1

Dear

IHT Mitigation

Now that we are beginning to see how much is going to be involved in setting up your IHT mitigation scheme, and learning that you would like me to organise everything, I think we need to address the subject of our fees at this stage.

As I see it, the work is going to involve regular and detailed correspondence, meetings, etc. I can either charge by the hour (which I think is never fair to the client – you never know what the bill is going to be until it arrives), or I can set a fee which would cover everything.

To give you some idea of what I have in mind, I think that in the next (say) six months, I am probably going to have a great deal of very responsible work to do. I estimate that my time will be 15 hours per month at our charge-out rate of £100 per hour. The fee on that basis would be £9,000. Now, in case we take less time than I am anticipating, what I propose to do is to discount this by 20 per cent and call the fee £7,200 (or £1,200 per month).

The fee is intended to cover *everything* apart from fees raised by other professionals and other advisers, but particularly it will cover:

- all correspondence, phone calls, etc. – so that you can phone at any time knowing that you are not being charged specifically for that call, letter, etc.
- all meetings, whether held here, Cornwall or in London
- travelling and out-of-pocket expenses
- controlling the process
- making sure all of your IHT mitigation strategies are put in place

My gut feeling is that this is a fair fee for the service involved and the tax saving on offer, but would you be happy? If this is in order then I would issue the fee note including VAT for this on 1 March with the suggestion that you pay it by standing order over the six months, starting 1 April 200x.

In return, if I fail to 'come up with the goods' then, obviously, you will be entitled to our usual guarantee of every penny you have paid being fully refundable.

Does this make sense?

Yours sincerely

Example 2

Dear

Setting up your Limited under the Enterprise Investment Scheme

You have asked me to write to you about the above proposal because not only is there need for some urgency but, with such a significant potential tax saving available to you, we need to agree a fee for this service at the outset.

I estimate that it will take about 30 working hours each month between now and the end of January to see this matter through to completion in time. Our standard charge-out rate for this is £120 per hour, which on this basis would result in a fee of £10,800 + VAT. However, when looking at a service like this, in case we take less time than anticipated, we always discount the fee by 20 per cent, so that our fees would be reduced to £8,640 – this brings the total fee including VAT to £10,152.00

For this we will:

- make the necessary amendments to the company's structure, including increasing the authorised share capital to £¼ million.
- advise you on the steps to take, and the order in which to take them, paying special attention to the timings and percentages.
- deal with Companies House to clear all the above matters
- deal with all the HMRC form-filling (including the EIS forms)
- deal with HMRC over this matter taking it to its successful completion
- get the relevant Revenue clearance for the scheme, together with the appropriate authorisation.

- issue the relevant forms
- issue the shares
- make the claim for the very substantial capital gains tax refund which will be due to you.
- in due course, make the claim to take your losses back against your last years of employment income. As you are already aware, this will result in a further substantial tax refund for you.
- if you wish, we would also register you for VAT so that, amongst other things, you could claim back the VAT of £1,512.00 on our fees for this service.

I do not think this will happen but, if we were to fail to get the company registered under the EIS scheme, there would be no fee for you to pay, no matter how many hours we had spent.

In addition you should note that:
- our fee will cover all meetings, telephone calls, correspondence, etc., whether held in your or HMRC's offices
- it will also cover all out-of-pocket expenses, including travelling

In other words, ours is an all-inclusive fee.

If this is acceptable, perhaps you would give me a call and we will put the process in motion at once. As you will appreciate, time is now pretty tight if we are to get this through in time.

Yours sincerely

Thoughts for members of the office team on dealing with client complaints

Sometimes, when a client complains, it is not dealt with in the first instance by a partner. When this happens, either a message is written down for the partner to deal with on his return, or, worse still, the message is handed-in verbally to the partner.

When the partner returns to the office with (usually) a stack of things that have to be done, the customer complaints are the last things that he wants to deal with instantly, as he is only human.

What I would like to do is to empower any team member who finds him or herself dealing with a complaint to deal with the complaint, scotch that complaint, and if possible make things better than they were before the phone call complaining about our failing arrived. I would like the person who is listening to the complaint to consider it as being their responsibility, even though they may have had nothing whatsoever to do with the cause of the problem.

In other words, I would like to empower everybody to do whatever is necessary to deal with the complaint the moment it arrives. It may mean saying sorry, it may be putting into effect an action that should have been taken sooner, and it may mean that we may need to look at the systems that gave rise to the complaint. It might well involve the arrangement of sending of flowers. It might mean 'doing their tax return for nothing'. Whatever it is, I want the team member to feel fully authorised to say sorry as fulsomely and as positively as possible.

The result of this 'instant' apology and putting matters right will be that our clients will become amazed at how quickly we make amends for our shortcomings and they will be even more impressed. Client x is now closer to us after our getting her postcode wrong (again) than she was before we/I goofed. If we don't institute this change, by the time the partner gets round to apologising and putting the matter right, the client will have probably dragged our name through the mud with eleven other people (whether clients or not), and the damage caused by the delay will have cost us significantly more than the granting of this 'empowerment'.

(By the way the dragging our name through the mud with 11 other people is not an invention of mine. It is a statistic that, if you are fed up with an organisation you are going to tell 11 other people. If you are delighted with an organisation you are likely to tell only three).

If we need to consider changing our systems as a result of receiving the complaint then whoever is responsible for that system should be told of the matter as soon as possible.

Obviously if it is a question of a technical matter then you will not be in a position to put the matter right instantly, but most complaints are due to the 'little things' and I think that this 'empowerment' will apply to the majority of customer complaints.

I hope you are happy with this.

HELP SHEET 11
Letter to a prospective client telling them what their fees will be

Dear

Thank you very much indeed for calling to see us and as promised, I am now itemising our services, together with the relevant fees. As you will have gathered from our meeting, we have a wide range of services but, if we have understood your wishes correctly, you wish us to attend to the following, for which our fee would be £1,000 plus VAT.

So long as the fee is paid on time it includes:
- Partnership Accounts preparation to 31 January 2007
- Our 2007 tax return service for you
- All telephone calls, correspondence, emails, faxes, etc.
- Our guarantee that if you are not satisfied with our service (and you are the only judge), you don't pay.

If what we are proposing is acceptable perhaps you would kindly fill in the enclosed letter in the appropriate manner and return it to us in the Freepost envelope so that we can set up your file – and be ready to do all the things that we promised. Thank you again for giving us this opportunity to quote and we hope that we will find ourselves able to be of service to you.

With best wishes.

Yours sincerely

HELP SHEET 12

The pro-forma letter for clients to sign and return in response to a quote from us

From: *(The new client)*

To: *(The accountant)*

Dear Sirs

I accept your quote for the fees and guarantees you have listed.

Please set up the relevant files and act accordingly.

My tax reference number is _____

My National Insurance number is _____

Yours faithfully

HELP SHEET 13
Spreadsheets that help you control the billing process

> If you use this idea, don't forget to enclose a Freepost envelope.

In our office we now keep two spreadsheets that bring this whole process together and you might like to see how we lay them out. (For reasons of space I have simplified this Help Sheet – as you will see this spreadsheet needs many more clients and many more services etc)

First of all, have a quick look at Helpsheet 4. There you will see the list of a whole range of services and what needs to happen is for the quotes (the prices) that you have sent out to be collated in a single spreadsheet, as follows.

To show you how this first sheet is prepared we will assume you have just three clients (two private individuals: Smith and Hamilton, and a limited company called Mercer Ltd.) and you provide five services (tax return, accounts, audit, payroll and company secretarial).

So the first spreadsheet would be laid out as follows:

20xx Fee Plan

Client	Tax return	Accounts	Audit	Payroll	Company Secretarial	Total
	£	£	£	£	£	£
Employee responsible for billing						
	Tim	Andrew	George	Martin	Reginald	
Smith	400					400
Hamilton	350	1,000		600	250	2,200
Mercer Ltd	500	5,000	5,750	1,500	250	13,000
Mercer Ltd Director A	250					250
Mercer Ltd Director B	250					250
TOTALS	£1,750	£6,000	£5.750	£2,100	£500	£16,100

continued overleaf

The particular benefits of using this kind of spreadsheet include that:

- You can tell quickly how many clients you have.
- You can tell how much you expect each department to earn. And the figures are based on real fees, not some hoped-for projection.
- You can tweak the figures before you send the advanced notice of fees (Helpsheet 4) out. It is so simple to increase fees by a few percentage points. The sort of tweak that makes a significant difference to your bottom line and your bank balance.
- You can give the responsibility for billings to your department heads. You, as a partner, hardly even need look at fees again, except once a year when you are making the fee budget for the next year.
- This spreadsheet will become the starting point for the following year's fee plan.
- If a client arrives or leaves, it's easy to see what affect their arrival or departure will have on your budget.
- The figure at the bottom right-hand corner (the total fees you anticipate billing) will be a very good starting point for you when it comes to budgeting.
- This spreadsheet shows you the blanks you have in the fee plan – so it might encourage you to market (say) payroll services to those for whom you are not doing this work.

But, having created this plan you need to chart the firm's billing progress against the targets you have now set. So here is the second spreadsheet, in this case taking the progress of your billing to the end of June:

Summary of Fee notes issued in 20xx

Client	Tax return	Accounts	Audit	Payroll	Company Secretarial	Total
	£	£	£	£	£	£
	Employee responsible for billing					
	Tim	Andrew	George	Martin	Reginald	
April	1,750			500		2,250
May					250	250
June		1,000				1,000
July						
August						
September						
October						
November						
January						
February						
March						
Running totals	£1,750	£1,000	£0	£500	£250	£3,500
Target	£1,750	£6,000	£5.750	£2,100	£500	£16,100

FURTHER READING

The Professional's Guide to Value Pricing by Ron Baker
(Panel Publishing, 2005: ISBN 0735548064)

Further Up the Organisation by Robert Townsend
(Hodder & Stoughton, 1985: ISBN 0340377577)

True Professionalism: The Courage to Care About Your People, Your Clients and Your Career by David Maister
(The Free Press, 2000: ISBN 0684840049)

The 7 Habits of Highly Effective People by Stephen Covey
(Free Press, 2004: ISBN 0743269519)

What Matters Most: The Power of Living Your Values by Hyrum Smith
(Free Press, 2001: ISBN 0684872579)

Clients are People Too! by James Alexander
(Management Books, 2000: ISBN 1852523549)

ACKNOWLEDGEMENTS

It can be dangerous thanking people for helping you write a book because there's a risk that no sooner is the book published than you realise that you have forgotten to thank someone, and that might be a vital someone – so, please forgive any omissions.

My thanks are due to:

Leo Ingenhaag, who first showed me that upfront billing can be done.

Paul Dunn and Rick Payne, who showed me that it must be done.

Tim Smith and all who work and have worked in my office and who have supported me with implementing this change in policy at HM Williams.

Our clients, who not only accepted but now totally endorse the fact that fixed fees have to replace billing by the hour.

Martin Gwynne, a chartered accountant of many years standing, who told me how tremendously important it is for the message in this book to get out.

Chris Peel, who bravely allowed me to give my two lectures on upfront billing to members of the Tax Faculty of the Institute of Chartered Accountants in England and Wales.

Mark Lee, former chairman of the Tax Faculty – not only for agreeing to write the Foreword but for so kindly and persistently singing the praises of this idea.

Indeed everyone who works in the Tax Faculty, past and present, who have been such incredible supporters of my efforts in this regard. I think of Francesca Lagerberg, Nina Turner and all the other friendly ladies and men, particularly Paul Aplin, whose support I have found immensely reassuring.

Those 20 or so practices that have bought into the idea of upfront billing and helped prove that it's an immensely practical and beneficial one.

David Hunt for reading it and saying, in effect, 'Publish and be damned.'

Anne Odling-Smee and Jaakko Tuomivaara of O-SB Design for making sure that this book looks as good as I like to think it is, and particularly thanks to Anne for introducing me to…

Ally Ireson, the editor, who has made sure that the contents of this book are a vast improvement on the original manuscript.

ABOUT ST EDWARD'S PRESS

St Edward's Press began publishing with a calendar of Saints Days in 1993. The company operates according to the credo 'An Independent and Different Approach' and thereby aims to produce books on subjects that are unlikely to be taken up by mainstream publishers.

Forthcoming titles

A Family at War
The diaries of the members of one family who fought in World War I, edited into a moving book that keeps the reader gripped to the very end – who will and won't make it to Armistice Day?

The EU and You
A book that describes in user-friendly style how the workings and decisions of the European Union affect each of and every one of us.

Martha Andreasen – My Story
The personal story of a former Chief Accountant at the European Commission who was sacked after she blew the whistle on serious discrepancies in the EU's accounts – a vital read for anyone who cares about democracy and about probity in public life.

History Fact Finder
A lively reference book that is written in chronological order with accompanying quick-reference sections, building a fascinating and yet very practical account of the story of world history.

Let Us Look To Our Moat
Vice Admiral Sir Louis Le Bailly on Britain's defences in the 21st century.

HOW TO ORDER THIS BOOK

If this particular copy of the book does not belong to you and you would like to buy a copy of your own, either photocopy the page overleaf or (with the owner's permission!) tear the sheet out, fill it in and post it to us at:

St Edward's Press
Freepost RRBC-SUZR-LUBK
Yelverton
Devon
PL20 7PS

Or fax it to us on 01822 859270

Alternatively, you can email your order to us at info@stedwardspress. co.uk, or make your order via the website, at www.stedwardspress.co.uk

Prices (including postage & packing)
1 copy	£20.00
2 copies	£30.00 (a 25 per cent discount)
5 copies	£60.00 (a 40 per cent discount)
10 copies	£100.00 (a 50 per cent discount)

Our no-quibble guarantee is that if you are not happy with your purchase, return the order to us with proof of payment for a full refund.

ORDER FORM

Your details

Please send me _____ copies of *Life without Timesheets*

My name is _____

Please send my order to me at

_____

_____

_____ Postcode _____

Telephone _____ Email _____

Paying by cheque

I enclose a cheque for £_____ *Make cheques payable to St Edwards Press Ltd*

Paying by credit card

Card number _____

Name on card _____

Type of card _____ Expiry date _____ / _____

Security number (last three numbers) on reverse of card _____

Signature _____ Date _____

Send your order to:
Freepost
RRBC-SUZR-LUBK
St Edward's Press Ltd
Yelverton PL20 7PS

Fax your order to:
01822 859270

Email your order to:
info@stedwardspress.co.uk